this is like that

poems and process

mandy monath

 f·e·a·r·l·e·s·s·w·o·r·d·s·p·u·b·l·i·s·h·i·n·g

For information, write to Fearless Words Publishing,
734 W. 2nd St., Washington, North Carolina 27889.

ISBN 979-8-218-07546-0

Cover and Interior Design: KUHN Design Group

Cover Art: *Wild Teasel*, by Barbara Garwood.
Pastel on mounted UART sanded paper. 8" x 6"

For Rob Monath

Man delights in seeing likenesses …
Observing each, he perceives and understands that this is like that.

Aristotle, ***Poetics***

CONTENTS

this is like that

GEESE

In eight lanes of rumble and tick
whine and click of engines halt
and go
I don't know
how I heard them

They flew so high
and few,
needing to,
surged so
on fleshy wings
into the darkening sky

Their animal voices found me
amid the jumble and snarl
the accidental human ugliness
like a baby's wail reaches its mother

I'd been waiting for a poem,
that lull, a gap
that comes in secret
and separates itself from the rest of the day.
I'd been waiting for the thing that stays.

DRIFT

A sliver of shade at the water's edge
uneasy refuge:
pendulous vines
trees too far off the perpendicular
old rumors of a hornets' nest

The dark water dimples,
current unseen
laps the red bank slick,
nudges the bow to ground.

There is no anchor,
no settling in.
Pull and drift are subtle
and constant.

In a spot of sun
wild roses blink,
wreathe a tree, pulled down at last,

its massive foot
upended slab of weathered root and burl
pocked with dark holes—
caves in a rocky place.

In the deepest
sleeps
a snake—
draped, luxurious,
sleek as a loaded gun.

This is your book now. Wander around in it. Write or sketch in it (unless it belongs to the library). Read some, then go take a walk. Watch and listen. Stay open for the poem that's looking for you.

Barbara Garwood's painting on the cover, *Wild Teasel*, is wildly beautiful, but the plant itself has a bad reputation. It's prickly, invasive, and hard to get rid of. In other words, it's a lot like a poem.

IT HAPPENS

It happens here
where five roads X their acrid tar,
a clutch of asphalt
Nothing worth the ER
no teddy bears or crosses
just fender-bending
vehicular rear-ending

The drivers
raw and inconvenienced
press into their phones
against the coming roar and heavy air
the piss of punctured radiators

It happens.
Someone blinks
or jumps the gun

Today the cop on duty
fails to factor in
the corner stand of myrtles
emanating since frost
a deafening crash of coral and green, throb
of unexpected joy
something to believe in.

MAP

The shape of the lake
eludes you.

Where is your place
in relation to that cove
that cup of cool
shifting on the other side.

It looks so close from here.
From there, here
looks so far away.

You've spread the map,
placed your finger on the bank,
stretched your hand across
to see what it is
you always see. But still
your place eludes you.

One small lake—
even one small stone
speckled in an endless list of coordinates—
is as hard to know
as another's heart,
as hard to know as your own.

Poetry, like painting or any art, begins with a catalyst. The smell of cedar fills the air. The sun shifts and lights up a tree. Something touches you, invades, and demands that you pay attention.

A moment strikes you and makes you feel.
William Wordsworth said poetry begins with a "spontaneous
overflow of powerful feelings." What struck you today?

MILKY WAY

Out in the dark road
hill and creek on either side because you feel them there
eye waist foot level all
black

thick mountain darkness
undiluted by any bright
fills your wide blindness with water
and all you can look
is up
where single lights
feed your eyes from more stars
than you ever knew

"You can really see the Milky Way."
That's what people say and you look
up for the white swirl you've seen in books
but how can you see it when you're in it

You tilt your face to more stars than you ever knew
spilled across the sky
from rim to rim
and now you can feel
where it is
and where you are
like looking down a long hall
to the other end of your house
that swims and rotates around you
swimming and rotating inside it

PALIMPSEST

In my landscape
brave and new
my home is square,
triangle roof,
stick and circle make a tree
Above, the sky hangs midnight blue,
below, the earth lies flat and green.

I'm left to wander in between,
unimpeded by eager gypsies
strange parades for lesser saints
shops closed at noon
lovely superfluity.
Craving spires
and ruins
grottoes steeped
in subterranean gloom
I wander through the neat and groomed.

Lovers busy underneath
an ancient arch
don't need elaborate boss
or heed it
The novice
long since bored by pricked-out eaves
sweeps the marble steps and flees.
Put here
—so unadorned—
they'd quickly feel the loss, and mourn.

As I click my narrow gate again at home
a breeze
half-conscious, fresh
from circling round the globe
maybe bearing mint or ash or brine
or tinkling rings of silver spoons and glass,
having swirled around a dome
or whispered wise
across an oculus
finds my heart, my mind,
my palimpsest.

ALMOST

Unlike the highway—
blasting and slashing
straight through these mountains,
breaking the hills—

this smaller road,
barely a road,
rises and falls
on the breast and curve of the earth.

Sometimes it runs to gravel
rasping under your tires,
and slopes of a sudden
into a clutch of homes,
a church, a store—
some place named Mineral or Apple.

On the highway, no signs point to Mineral
or Apple—
but you could almost
live out your life here.

You could crouch on a wide rock
in the middle of a stream,
trail your fingers
in a velvet pour of cold white water,
spot a speckled trout,
watchful in a pool of shade.

You could try to number
the lichens and mosses, the earthy mushrooms,
fixed in the doty flesh of one fallen oak.

You could burst between your teeth
the skins of dark berries that
fringe the edge of a bright field—
or bring them to her door,
hat in hand.

You could fill a barn with summer hay,
pull a sweet blossom from the tangled bales.

You could kneel
and work between your fingers
the fresh soil that feeds you.
The same soil
that receives you
after a full and astonishing life
in Mineral or Apple.

SWANS

It worries the edge of your seeing:
a gleam of unusual white
winking
far out on the margin
The odd thing
that catches the eye
    a gallon milk jug lodged
    bobbing
    in the mud
    broken chunks of Styrofoam
No.

Swans
to be sure
a pair of immaculate swans

For weeks they stay
and daily
pull your helpless gaze
like the welder's white-hot flame
as white as a novel star, as white
as the glowing robes of Jesus

Then one hollow afternoon
the strand is bare
The pair is gone

In the fading light
nothing separates the deep
from land or sky—
all gray—
as though the doubting world had never
seen the Third or Second Day

You turn for home
your path the same
like swans
that yearly round an ancient gyre

At home
you bank the fire
You light your lamps
and wait.

EARLY

Sometime after Hesiod's winter
    when the north wind
    can pierce the hide of an ox
    bend an old man like a wheel

    when the tender girl
    in the warmest room of the house
    washes her soft body
    and anoints her skin with oil—

after that—
but well before spring splits
the wood
and drives the gaudy flower,
bare limbs
brighten
and change their way
of bathing in light

Something liminal
imminent
    a thin wisp of purple smoke
hovers
over the redbud
like a prophecy

Often, we ignore the poetic catalyst. We have other things to
do. But somewhere in us. in our artist brain, the experience
sticks and lives whole. It's as hard to get rid of as wild teasel. It
needles us and demands to be examined and understood.

The catalyst isn't the poem. For Wordsworth,
a strong feeling has to be "recollected in tranquility."
Poets need space and time to recall and reflect.

PAINTING

I wasn't there
when you felt the sun
setting fire to the hedge of forsythia
or when you noticed the startling colors
in the neat grass beneath your feet

I didn't sense the importance
of that line
that holds
between our arrangement of nature
and nature unarranged
That dark tangle of woods
beyond the hedge
That hint of infinite sky

But taking this frame
into my hands
Now I do.

TRY

Try to remember the tiny crab,
white claws
rocking to its mouth,
grasping eating grasping eating:
an urge that doesn't flicker through the mind
but lives in claws and meat.

Remember the sudden sideways scuttle,
the bigger claw held like a fiddle.
What's a fiddle? says the crab.
What's its name? says the child.
We don't name animals in the wild,
an old woman says, her hair down to her waist.
What's a fiddle?

Adam named the animals
not for pleasure
but to place them, like with like,
according to the law apportioned to each.
The shark eats the big fish,
the big fish—and so on—
each according to its kind.
The sea star pushes its stomach through a crevice
in the clam's shell and digests the clam.
Not even claw to mouth:
One life simply comprehends the other.

Remember to sense again
the pungent flats,
the snap of shrimp
vanished in a flash from the dimpled
black mud.
Recall the power of boundless spartina,
tawny and vast, speaking like speech itself:
Here I am. Here.
I am.

Try to remember the bright bird
quick and light, angled in the reeds.
And the baby alligator,
who already knows
the value
of perfect stillness.

THIS IS LIKE THAT

I.

In the half light
a ridge
rough and finger-deep
gives him again
the curved back of the bison

He scoops warm ashes from the dying fire
rubs them into the drip of hollowed stone
and blackens the spine
daubs in the legs where they go
then the head, bowed low
above the spot where the rock muscles.
At last, he makes the horns that gouge.

Scholars will wonder why but
in the almost light
he smiles
for the others to rise
and see
that this is like that

II.

The sharp flesh of your pencils
ochre and manganese
wear smooth on the paper's tooth

You too know
that the leaf on the page
is not the leaf in your hand
That
is pure color, walnut silk
curled and ruched along one side

Twirled between your fingers
it reaches into a spiral, swoops
and dives.

Such a small beautiful thing.

The details of this world are endless
in number
and full-blown being

You pick one out
to make it again on the page
To feel the joy
that this is like that.

MOON

What, on earth, do you say about the moon?
silver deity of secret night
love's guardian
A mirror, merely, in the evening sky
reflecting what shines
in the poet's iambic eye

Until
in the clear blue middle of the day
at noon
while you're leaning against your car
outside the Wasabi café,
the rough round rock of the moon
heavy and wild
crashes into view

Majestic and huge
raked by daylight
it startles and looms.
There all along
it feels completely new.

A scribbled note ('cedar') is enough to bring back a powerful memory for careful examination. At your writing table, you jot down every detail you can remember. What did you see, hear, smell, feel?

In the process, you'll get closer to answering the
most important question: Why did it matter?

CLEAR

This autumn morning
from my speeding car
I saw two people
old, and face to face.
He, black, she white
a yellow sweater
a fist of red
coxcombs
his hat was new
the sky was deep sky blue

DUSK

After the others have folded up
and gone
shrugged the immensity
of ocean and sky
for gate and roof

the sea parts and couples
like a bead of mercury
many and one
wobbly, Protean toy

molten surf shatters
the evening
tosses and spreads before me
shards
of sunset and cloud

the waves speak on,
even the horizon
taut and plumb
quivers at the lip of the world
and spills

Soon I'll follow the others home,
dump the puzzle out
and sort the pieces,
cottage from sea,
cloud from boat and sails:
    dark from light,
      furled from unfurled.

We'll work the edges first.

ENTROPY

Now the measuring cup
is gone,
the soft metal one with
quarters stamped into the side:
I need it.
And the wooden spoon
and the potholder
woven on a little loom.

How can you lose so much
in such a small space?

The children haul things off
to their parallel world
Socks and dolls, pots
blocks and spatulas
drift like flotsam
to the carpet's edge

No one's to blame
Things fall apart
    house, garden,
    heart
    the best laid plans
    at random
stars cool and die
the universe expands

Maybe chaos is just order
we don't understand.
A firefly teases through the yard
with a logic mysterious to me
On the ground, in the tree
On and off
lost, then found.
Like a lover, gone for years,
unpredictably back in town.

PEARL

Love
whether it is lost
wrong
wrongheaded
undeclared or
unrequited
is still
love

In a box of
found glass, shiny cubes
of pyrite, ticket stubs
buttons saved
subway tokens
loose charms
and small change from former nations

one loose
pearl
is still a pearl—
as round
and bright as the moon

"Poet" means "maker" in Greek. From your experience, you make a poem—a complete and intentional object presented to the reader to be unfolded and experienced in turn.

Painters use line, value, and color; poets, image, sound,
and rhythm, to create something thoroughly new.

SIX

She tumbles a somersault
on the rug, cuts
a wobbly cartwheel
For kicks
goes it one-handed
I'm in the circus!

The thing about being six—
the circus tent is open.
You can slip through
(canvas roughs your face)
and choose to spend your balance
in beautiful play
seize some magnificent purpose,
glad and holy

Later we pull down the tent
Store it, rolled neat,
poles snug in narrow sleeves
and forget the gaudy steed
pawing sawdust
at the edge of the ring
the one that was waiting
ready for anything.

FEAST

Wind huddles us
hard
by some nameless wood
scrawled black
against the frozen hill,
some scrub of trees,
quince or accidental
pear, tangled and bare
still hung with russet
fruit, small
and soft from frost.

Underfoot
puddles of slush,
scrim of ice
on a stubble
of grass,
break
the tired promise
of a snowy evening.

On the lake
thick with cold
one duck
dives long and again
for something gone.

Sleet ticks all around.
Now rain.

We start to shuffle home

then stop

and watch this wood
fill up with song.

One robin, then
a dozen,
hundred
more
clatter in, ring
the trees,
whirl, careen,
alight
on every twig and limb
to glean
the unexpected feast—

and sing.

Red notes
on a treble staff
they sing

Brightly shaken bells
they sing.

WATER

Rising from a hidden source
rivers furrow the earth
Seas shape or take an island
Drops hollow stone

But once come in, tide
lies all night
in curves of sand
closed in warm pools
and swimming
Rivers stay their beds
Poured into a vessel
water finds its form

A poet must gain the reader's confidence and be a reliable guide to the truth of the poem. The lyrical "I" of the poet doesn't say "Look at me." Instead, it says, "Come with me.'

Something in us (I'll call it soul) recognizes and
responds to something universal in the work of art.

PIANO

Under a soft single light
I and this piano sit upright

Knees touching knees
fingers and keys
cautious and delicious as new lovers

Soothing you
smoothing me
we almost sleep

LAST

If today were my last
I'd want more sunsets, obviously
and more love
and more of the soft curve of a child's face

But I'd take anything:

Carpool,
paperwork,
homework, in bad lighting,
at the dining room table,
before the dishes are cleared

It's what we have

So why not perch now
on this sweet trembling edge of time
steeped in gratitude?

It's no less
for not being last.

A poem balances play and focus. If the surface is too
busy, the reader ceases to trust you. If the poem
is too focused, it loses its joy and energy.

Anticipate your reader's skepticism and objections.
Lead in gradually. Prepare and persuade.

GEESE 2

It only takes
V after V
of geese
streaming
just over the trees,
ascending from some lake
to another

Or the green scent of cedar
from a tangle of branches
on a passing truck

Or a mockingbird
singing
anything

to crack the dome
of quiet desperation,
to put worry
—and words—
to shame.

MEMENTO MORI

Next to the hospital
is a cemetery.
Convenient
for that,
and for a little walk
beyond the thump
of mechanical breathing
the elevator's ping ping ping.

Huge oaks shade
the shades laid to rest before
the reign of the riding lawnmower
Determined roots
suck life between the mossy tombstones
nudged askew

One poet quips that he loves nature
especially if there's a hospital nearby
Here *memento mori* drones
against a trill of lilies
and a thousand sprouting acorns

In the sun
a neat hedge of privet
trimmed and square
hems the perimeter
unbroken
save for one delicate slit

I sidestep through it
crown into the roaring street

Not me.
Not today.

TROPE

I won't tell you much
about the bufflehead

I can say, in black and white,
his head is distinctive
he's the nattiest thing on the water
and the most buoyant:
dives forever and pops up
like a rubber ball clearing
the surface

A good poet once labeled
the cormorant a potbellied arrow,
which trope, ruinous and true,
sticks in my mind
whenever I see one fly.
Poor cormorant:
forever comic, undignified

So, I'll leave you
baffled by the bufflehead
not baffled precisely, more
innocent
innocent of the bufflehead
until you meet him yourself.

"Form is the getting from an accidental
beginning to a necessary end."

A.R. AMMONS

"Form is open to any beginning, but once it makes
several commitments, the end is necessary."
A.R. AMMONS

BULLDOZER MANIFESTO

Verba virumque cano, if I may.
Prose can be poetic but
poetry is not prose is not poetry
Poetry plays (see foregoing
allusion elision chiasmus alliteration)
Poetry is not prose cut up
into cute couplets
typography subbing for substance

Prose has work to do
Someone said the language of love is surely prose
I love you. Will you marry me? Not there, darling, here.
Prose can play but, in the end, must get the job done.
Who finishes Finnegan?

Speaking of allusions:
for best results, use sparingly
Don't hang your work like thin lingerie
on the sturdy bones of
Creatures from the sea!
Famous paintings!
Allude, with gratitude,
then grow bones of your own

One day I saw something gleam
like gold in the green
of a scrub pine tree
and flew at once to Aeneas
and his shiny bough.
Poetry needs beauty (the serious kind)
and all kinds of truth
but you can try too hard:

Sometimes
it's just a yellow bulldozer
parked under a pine tree

A poem delivers a stab
before its written,
and after,
which is the poet's job:
careful honing of the beautiful blade

Beautiful isn't the same as pretty
as the dead pheasant
beside the bloody rabbit
on the red tapestry
proved long ago
But neither is truth ugly:
A wobbly ill-balanced blade
hastily made and waved
in clumsy ambush
will miss its mark.
If you must write
about your private parts (by which I mean
one's privates, the universal
privates, as it were)
don't
unceremoniously
drop your drawers.
We hardly know you.

Poetry is art
not propaganda.
Learn the difference.
Put down your sign and listen
to the creative mind
as fine as your own
that speaks to you
across time

A poem can
lead us to the underworld,
speaking of allusions.
It leads the soul beneath
the pedestrian, the conscious,
through a maze of sense and guesses
leaps and surprises
until the soul says
Yes, I remember that now.

Sometimes a promising inspiration doesn't become a poem. Maybe it's too slight or too personal. It worked in my head but not on paper. Maybe it's a scrap that will someday fit into a larger piece. In any case, I try to move on. There's more to come.

ACKNOWLEDGMENTS

My sincere thanks to:

Barbara Garwood for *Wild Teasel* on the cover, for many conversations about the process of poetry and painting, and for bringing a painter's keen eye to these poems;

Louise Gossett for no-nonsense encouragement and insight;

the late A.R. Ammons for generous poetic wisdom;

Ardis Kimzey and the North Carolina Poetry in the Schools Program for introducing me to the joys of contemporary poetry;

NC State Poetry Contest (*Geese*, finalist 2006);

Editors at *Incunabula*, where earlier versions of *Piano* and *Milky Way* were published.

NOTE: The passage from Aristotle's *Poetics* on which the title is based can be found at 1448b 15-17.

ABOUT THE AUTHOR

Mandy Monath earned a B.A. from Salem College (Winston-Salem, North Carolina) in Classics and English, and an M.A. from UNC-Chapel Hill in Comparative Literature. Lyric poetry, with its evocative precision of language, has always been her favorite medium, but she has also published pieces in various newspapers, including *Christian Science Monitor* and *The Wall Street Journal*. Her plays, written with co-author Karin Gleiter, have been staged at the Raleigh (NC) Little Theater and the Carrboro (NC) Arts Center. Her short story *Home* won the Haunted Pamlico Horror Fiction Contest in 2021. Her children's story, *How Counting Came to Be*, will be published in Spring 2023. She divides her time between Raleigh and Washington, North Carolina. *This Is Like That* is her first poetry collection.

COVER ARTIST

Barbara Garwood earned a B.A. from UNC-Charlotte. She has studied pastel painting with Liz Haywood-Sullivan, Elizabeth Mowry and Karen Margulis (online). Barbara's work was juried into the North Carolina Statewide Pastel Exhibition in 2018, 2020 (when she received an Award of Excellence), and 2022. Barbara finds pastels both brilliant and subtle. She loves this medium for its immediacy in connecting with the surface and the spontaneity this allows. She lives in Salisbury, North Carolina.

www.ingramcontent.com/pod-product-compliance
Lightning Source LLC
Chambersburg PA
CBHW030517130626
46549CB00007B/3026

* 9 7 9 8 2 1 8 0 7 5 4 6 0 *